Frank Lloyd Wright
Design

Frank Lloyd Wright Design

Maria Costantino

BARNES
&NOBLE
BOOKS
NEW YORK

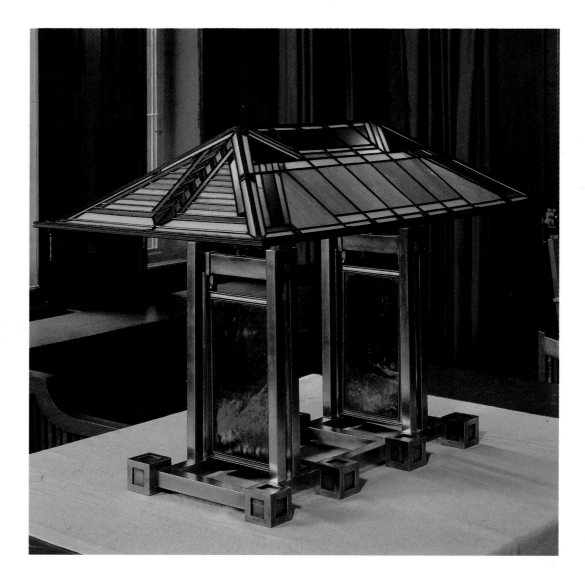

This edition published by
Barnes & Noble, Inc.,
by arrangement with Brompton Books Corporation.

Produced by Brompton Books Corporation,
15 Sherwood Place,
Greenwich, CT 06830

ISBN 1-56619-658-2

Printed in Spain

PAGE 1: The carved stone marking the entrance to Frank Lloyd
Wright's studio at Oak Park, Illinois.

PAGE 2: Clerestory windows light up the dining area of the
Melvyn Maxwell Smith House, Bloomfield Hills, Michigan.

ABOVE: Double pedestal lamp with sumac motif in the living
room of the Susan Lawrence Dana House, Springfield, Illinois.

Contents

Introduction

In the latter part of his career Frank Lloyd Wright was asked which of his buildings was he most pleased with, he replied, "the next one." This apparently flippant reply was, in fact, on announcement of the continuous process of evolution that Wright caused his work to undergo, during both the conceptional stages, and during actual building. Even after the projects were finished Wright continued to evolve his designs, often changing plans and publicity material.

This constant improvement of designs is apparent in a number of Wright's buildings, including his own home and studio at Oak Park, but can also be seen in the Isabel Roberts House, a Prairie House built in 1908. In 1955 the owners asked Wright's help with the restoration of the building. Rather than looking to the past and the original 1908 scheme, Wright evolved the Roberts's house into a contemporary house of the 1950s, in which the plasterwork ceilings were replaced with lapped mahogany boards and the stucco exterior changed to

brick. In short, there was no attempt at a pure restoration by Wright – the project was, for him, an opportunity to demonstrate his latest design innovations.

Wright's constant improvement of his designs also manifested itself in a near-compulsive habit of re-arranging the furniture of his Oak Park home in order to achieve better spatial compositions. This habit even extended to his clients' homes when, during subsequent visits, and often to their displeasure, Wright would rearrange their furniture to try out new spatial configurations and solutions. Wright's goal, whether in his residential commissions or in his large-scale commercial designs such as the Larkin Co. Administration Building or the S. C. Johnson & Son (Johnson Wax) Administration Building, was to create harmony between the building and its furnishings.

Throughout his career Wright was to develop a number of "variations on themes" which had their origins in a variety of sources, including Japanese and

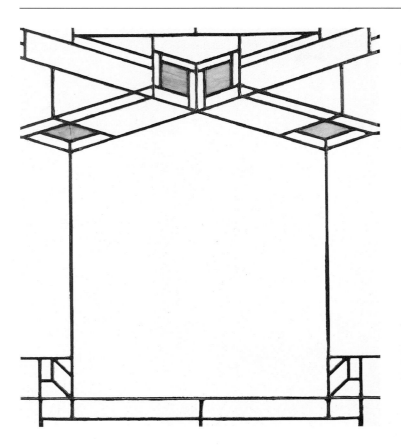

pre-Columbian designs, and geometric, abstracted forms that provided him with an ornamental vocabulary which, although highly stylized, was on the whole derived from nature and natural forms.

An early influence, and one frequently acknowledged by Wright himself, was his introduction as a child to Froebel's kindergarten "gifts." Froebel's kindergarten teaching system encouraged children to play but, without their realizing it, their play was transformed into a recognition and appreciation of natural objects. Children were offered toys as "gifts," and these gifts were simply shapes in primary colors, initially limited to three basic forms: the cube, the cylinder, and the sphere. The child-craftsman was taught to manipulate the shapes firstly

FACING PAGE: Frank Lloyd Wright c. 1909, already an established architect in the process of forming an indelible imprint on 20th-century design, including the decorative arts.

ABOVE LEFT: Window from the R. W. Evans House, Chicago, Illinois. Clear and translucent green glass in zinc cames, c .1908, 119 × 107 × 4.5 cm.

ABOVE RIGHT: The drafting-room balcony at the Frank Lloyd Wright Studio, suspended by chains from the roof beams and well lighted by clerestory windows.

RIGHT: Wright at work in 1945, surrounded by his apprentices.

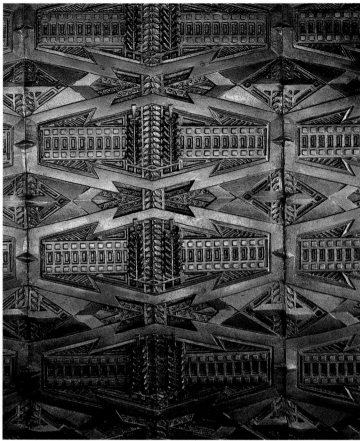

into two-dimensional patterns, and then into more complex three-dimensional constructions, which Froebel called "forms of life, of beauty and of knowledge." Through play children learnt that these simple constructions were the basis of all natural appearances.

For Wright, the two- and three-dimensional Froebel schemes and experiences were to exert a long-lasting influence on his approach to design, particularly his emphasis on the direct expression of function and simple forms. Wright rediscovered Froebel's "gifts" when he was about 25, and the subsequent influence of the children's building blocks can be seen in the George Blossom House, the Frederick C. Robie House, the Larkin Co. Administration Building, and Unity Temple.

Other influences grew out of Wright's early employment with the architects Joseph Lyman Silsbee and Louis Sullivan. Silsbee, a much sought-after designer of elegant "Shingle-Style" houses, had been commissioned by Wright's uncle, Reverend Jenkin Lloyd Jones, to design a new building for the All Souls' Church in Chicago. According to the story, Wright was introduced to Silsbee, and the next day was set to work on the new building, which was to resemble a clubhouse rather than a church with its informal asymmetric design, and mix of brickwork and brown shingle. While Wright remained with Silsbee for only seven or eight months, he would never forget Silsbee or the lessons he had learnt: in Wright's early works of the 1880s and 1890s, and later in the Usonian houses of the late 1930s and 1940s, the basis of Wright's work was the tendency to incorporate polygonal elements – elements that can be

traced back to Silsbee.

In the fall of 1887 Wright joined the firm of Adler & Sullivan which had just been awarded a highly coveted commission for the design of the Auditorium Building in Chicago. In addition to designing, Sullivan also wrote about his approaches to design and stated that the first source of inspiration was nature. The influence of Sullivan on Wright's later work is apparent in details of the Isidore Heller House (1896), particularly in the Sullivanesque ornamental frieze; in the William H. Winslow House (1893) in its use of the abstract motif of oak leaves, and in the design of the carved oak door which expresses Sullivan's idea of natural organic growth as the basis for good design. Further examples include the decorative details of the terra-cotta archway of the Francisco Terrace Apartments (1895), which is filled with foliage reminiscent of Wright's and Sullivan's portal for the Transportation Building built for the Chicago World's Fair in 1893.

Despite increasingly using geometric and abstract designs, his basis remained firmly rooted in nature, and Wright's concept of the "organic" nature of architecture soon included designing furnishings which would be integral to the structure in which they were housed. Possibly the most famous example of Wright's highly stylized ornamental designs are the windows for the Darwin D. Martin House (1904), in which Wright utilized a repetitive scheme of flowers and leaves, often referred to as the "tree of life" pattern.

The Martin House was the largest and most expensive residential project of Wright's Prairie House years, and

consisted of a house, a long gallery, a conservatory, and a gardener's cottage. Some of the art-glass windows were used in a decorative wall scheme in the reception area and filtered and transformed the sunlight, while other art glass formed part of the conservatory scheme, where a solid brass leading was specified in order to harmonize

with the greens and yellows of the conservatory color scheme and the plants. The "tree of life" design is also related to the ornamental relief on the pier capitals of 1903, designed by Wright for the Larkin Co. Administration Building, of which Darwin D. Martin was company secretary.

FACING PAGE, LEFT: An exterior sconce against the innovative reinforced concrete construction at Unity Temple, Oak Park, Illinois.

FACING PAGE, RIGHT: Detail of the nature-inspired exterior frieze at the Susan Lawrence Dana House, Springfield, Illinois.

ABOVE LEFT: The inglenook seating area and fireplace at the Frank Lloyd Wright Home in Oak Park. The motto above the fireplace surround was a feature of the Arts and Crafts style.

ABOVE RIGHT: A passageway lined with intricately-patterned art glass at the Susan Lawrence Dana House.

RIGHT: The dining room of the Susan Lawrence Dana House, in which the intricate light fixture at top right relates to the window design.

LEFT: The Avery Coonley House, built in 1907. Wright called this a "zoned" house, since the spacious site enabled him to spread the residence out in long wings commanding the landscaped grounds. The entire living area is on one level, raised above the ground to form the first floor. The space below comprises entry, playroom, and utilities.

Lighting was a very important part of Wright's architectural schemes, and he used a variety of sources, including natural light, which was filtered through skylights and windows, and artificial light provided by hanging lamps, desk and table lamps, and wall sconces. In 1895 Wright remodeled his own house, adding a playroom, a new kitchen, and a dining room. It was also the first occasion upon which he designed all the furnishings, and where the ceiling light was of an enclosed, indirect electric-light type.

The Susan Lawrence Dana House (1902) was a project in which Wright was given an absolutely free hand, with no budgetary constraints. In the entrance, a spectacular display of art glass sets the tone for the entire house with

LEFT: Wright, aged 87, points out features of the Frederick C. Robie House, built in 1906, in an attempt to prevent the demolition of the house in 1957. The architect and his supporters prevailed, and the house became a national landmark as Wright's best expression of the Prairie-style masonry structure.

its magnificent decorative features. More art glass is to be found in the lamps in the dining room, in a liquor cabinet with leaded glass doors, and in the magnificent glass doors with their stylized wisteria motif which link the reception area with a rear hallway. Said to be the finest that Wright ever designed, the doors were made by the Linden Glass Co. of Chicago.

Often Wright would use the same designs or variations of them in different buildings: the same rectilinear design of the wall sconces that were used in the Dana House turn up again in the Little House I (1903), where the iridescent green and amber glass was in perfect harmony with the Prairie-style earth colors favored by Wright. A second light sconce, this time used throughout much of the interior of the Avery Coonley House (1907), has its cover plate perforated in a geometric pattern which is visible both from above and below. Again based on natural forms, this time the abstract pattern is derived from fern leaves, a motif which occurs again in the ceiling of the living room, and in the fireplace mural painted by George Niedecken. The same light sconce was used in other Wright projects of the same date, such as the Frederick C. Robie House and the Meyer May House.

Unity Temple (1904) makes use of an interior skylight, and integrates the visual aspects of a building with the structural: the ceiling beams which run north-south are solid and serve as supports for the roof, while the east-west running beams are, in fact, hollow, and provide the pattern for the ceiling.

In addition to the nature-inspired motif such as the "tree of life" pattern, or the highly stylized motifs of

prairie flora such as sumac (a native Illinois plant which can be seen again in the Dana House in the exterior ornamental frieze), Wright also drew on European, pre-Columbian and Oriental sources. Over 60 years Wright produced 15 variations of the high-backed dining chair,

ABOVE RIGHT: A corner of the living room of the Meyer May House, showing a rocking chair, art glass, and a wall sconce. This most beautifully restored of all Wright's Prairie houses shows his masterful integration of space for both private and community life.

RIGHT: The gallery of the Susan Lawrence Dana House, the first of Wright's houses to contain two-story rooms. The gallery served as a reception area and is connected to the house by a covered passage. The dining room and the hall are also two stories high.

LEFT AND BELOW: Wright's Imperial Hotel, Tokyo. The hotel survived the Tokyo earthquake in 1923, but was demolished in 1968. The hotel was designed to have a low center of gravity, with balanced loads supported by cantilevered reinforced concrete slabs – a concept entirely new to Japanese architecture.

FACING PAGE, BELOW: A specially designed chair, *c.* 1935, for the hotel. It was a six-year project for which Wright designed all the carpets, textiles, furniture, and tableware.

running from the first-known designs done in solid oak for his own dining room in 1895, to those produced in plywood for the Lovness House in 1955.

Although most of the chair backs have square spindles, some do have slats or even solid back panels. On some, the backs run into the seat, in others they run halfway down while, in others, they terminate at floor level and have a highly architectonic feel to them. The original high-backed chairs serve as the earliest of this type of design in America, and in some respects are stylistically similar to those designed in 1900 by the Scottish architect Charles Rennie Mackintosh for Miss Cranston's tearooms in Glasgow.

Wright would have been familiar with Mackintosh's and other European designers' work through journals such as *The House Beautiful*. Yet where Mackintosh

made frequent use of painted surfaces, especially white, and ornamental inlays, Wright consistently used natural-finish oaks. As with most of Wright's furniture, the forms harmonize with the architecture for which they were designed. For the square-plan Arthur Heurtley House (1902), Wright designed a square-form reclining armchair with tapering armrests and front legs set at an angle which correspond to the projecting window bay in the dining room, as well as to the angular arrangements of the living room itself.

Other European influences can be seen in designs for the Midway Gardens (1913) and the Avery Coonley Playhouse (1912). In 1909 Wright traveled to Europe where he spent two years, and many of his designs on his return show that he had learned of the experiments in abstraction that were being caried out by many of the European avant-garde artists and designers. The Avery Coonley Playhouse, so called because it contained a small stage in the building designed to serve as a kindergarten, contained windows displaying two-dimensional abstract designs which were based on Wright's observations of a parade with balloons and flags. While the colorful designs were completely appropriate for a kindergarten, they were also Wright's first nonobjective geometric designs, and were possibly influenced by artists like Robert Delaunay and František Kupka, whose works he would no doubt have seen during his stay in Europe.

In the fall of 1913 Wright was commissioned to create a pleasure garden near the University of Chicago. The Midway Gardens were to have a number of spaces, both indoor and outdoor, for dining, dancing, and concerts, and offered Wright the opportunity to design a magnificent architectural complex as well as all the interior fixtures and fittings, right down to the ceramic place settings. Of the small number of pieces to survive the demolition of the Midway Gardens in 1929, a glazed porcelain plate is decorated simply, with a fine line and a single row of red squares around the edge of the plate and a cartouche with the Midway Gardens device. The decorative red squares on the plates were, in fact, a motif frequently used by Josef Hoffmann and other Viennese Secessionist designers, which Wright may have seen in design magazines or perhaps while in Europe. In other parts of the Midway Gardens, sculptures executed by Wright's assistants Alfonso Iannelli and Richard Bock recall the work of the Cubists; the overlapping horizontal and vertical planes of the "Sprite" sculptural decorations do not appear in Wright's work prior to his trip to Europe.

Wright's interest in non-European art forms came from his first employer, Silsbee, who was an avid collector of "Orientalia." The fashion for *Japonisme* that had been cultivated in Europe since the 1860s by artists such as Whistler had slowly filtered through to avant-garde Americans. But the first large-scale introduction to

the American Midwest of Japanese art and design came at the Chicago World's Fair in 1893. During the time that the firm of Adler & Sullivan — with whom Wright was employed — was working on the Transportation Building, Wright made several trips to the fair where there was a Japanese *Ho-o-den*, a half-scale replica of a Fujiwara-period wooden temple, on show. In 1905, Wright (accompanied by his first wife, Catherine, and his clients Mr. and Mrs. Ward W. Willits) made his first trip to Japan, where his interest in Oriental art and design grew. On his return to the United States, Wright began to collect Japanese prints, and often advised his clients on their purchases. From Japanese prints Wright claimed to have learned of the elimination of insignificant details, which led him to simplify his design.

One of Wright's greatest architectural achievements was the Imperial Hotel in Tokyo, Japan. Like the Midway Gardens the Imperial Hotel was a large complex that was unified by Wright's working of the decorative scheme, including the design of all the interior details — furniture, ceramics, carpets, flatware, and textiles. Although Wright began the designs for the hotel in 1915 and construction began two years later, the project was not completed until 1922. (Although the Imperial Hotel emerged relatively intact following the great 1923 earthquake, and was largely undamaged during World War II, during the early years of the American

occupation of Japan the hotel was altered by the U.S. military. In 1968 the hotel was demolished, but the entrance lobby was dismantled and reconstructed in 1976 at the Meiji Village, a museum to the west of Tokyo.)

In designing the hotel and its furnishings, Wright created a cohesive unity through the use of geometric forms, such as the hexagonal backs of the side chairs, the shape of which was repeated in the table tops and in the ceiling decoration of the central lounge. (A variation of this hexagonal-backed chair occurs again later, with Wright's custom-designed furniture for the Harold C. Price Co. Tower apartments in Oklahoma in 1952.) The overall design of the carpets for the main dining room of the hotel reflected the architecture of the building: Wright utilized traditional Japanese masonry by the incorporation of castellated profiles constructed in brick dressed with oya – a sort of lava stone – while the circular-motif decoration on the chinaware is also reminiscent of both the designs for the windows of the Avery Coonley Playhouse and of Nabashima-ware, a type of eighteenth-century Japanese porcelain.

Japanese art and design were to continue to exert an influence on Wright throughout his career, as is evident in many of his later designs for furniture in the Usonian projects, like the Paul J. Trier House (1956), and even in Wright's own home at Taliesin West (1937-59), which features "origami" chairs, the arms of which give the impression that they can be folded up, but which are actually stationary and braced at the back.

Wright had long been interested in pre-Columbian architecture. At the Chicago World's Fair he had seen a partial reconstruction of the Mayan Nunnery at Uxmal, as well as other Mayan buildings, and in the Midway Gardens project Wright adopted the approach of placing

an ornamental band of geometric motifs, being directly inspired by Mayan and Zapotec examples above plain masonry surfaces.

Pre-Columbian themes were to be developed further in 1917, when Wright shifted his work base from Chicago to Los Angeles. The major attraction that southern California had for Wright was that the area had the feel of a "desert" that could be transformed by irrigation and by the construction of planned cities. Furthermore, Wright saw the area as both factually and mythically linked to a primitive pre-Columbian culture. Because the art of the Mayans and Zapotecs originated in the Americas, Wright could also use the style to emphasize the cultural independence of the New World from Europe. Since these historic cultures were associated with Mexico and, by extension, with the Hispanic regions of the southwestern states of America, Wright's pre-Columbian-inspired designs appeared "right" for the area, seemingly growing organically out of the landscape.

Wright's first building in California, the George C. Stewart House (1909) in Montecito is, however, essentially a Prairie House transplanted to a radically different environment; nevertheless, it does demonstrate the flexibility of the Prairie House scheme. Only later, in 1917, in the concrete Aline Barnsdall House (Hollyhock

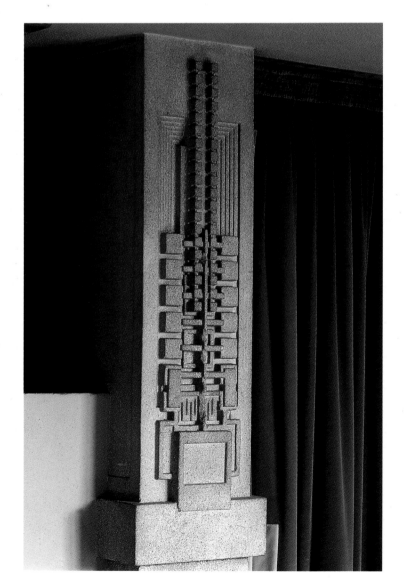

LEFT: A salad plate designed by Wright for the Imperial Hotel, and manufactured by Noritake.

BELOW LEFT: The hollyhock motif that features prominently in the Aline Barnsdall House.

RIGHT: Detail of the skylight above the hearth in the Aline Barnsdall House.

BELOW: The interior of the Charles Ennis House, the most imposing of the four Los Angeles textile-block houses. Lloyd Wright worked on this house with his father and designed the landscaping.

BELOW RIGHT: Detail from a concrete block in the Charles Ennis House.

House), was the Mayan influence fully displayed. Repeated throughout the Barnsdall House is an abstract hollyhock-flower-and-trellis motif: it is found on the exterior concrete-frieze decoration, in the light fixtures, in the glass for the windows, on the dining-room walls, and on the backs of the dining chairs, where the flower buds are transformed into small squares.

Since the turn of the century, Wright, along with other avant-garde architects, had proposed concrete, precast concrete blocks and cement stucco sheathing as new materials suitable for domestic architecture. The combined house and studio for Alice Madison Millard, La Miniatura (1923), was Wright's first textured concrete-block house in California. Situated in a valley surrounded by trees and overlooking a pond, the house has a two-story living room with a window wall of glass doors at the lower level, and pierced concrete blocks above. The thin concrete blocks, with their cross pattern suggestive of the pre-Columbian architecture at Oaxaca in Mexico, occur both on the external walls and inside, thereby uniting the exterior with the interior.

Three other textured concrete-block houses in southern California were designed by Wright in the 1920s: the John Storer House (1923), the Charles

Ennis House (1923), and the Freeman House (1923-24), all of which display pre-Columbian influences, although in the last house these are combined with a new theme of Islamic motifs, such as in the use of perforated interior screens instead of heavy masonry walls – a method that recalls Mogul architecture.

Like other architects, such as Louis Sullivan, Wright used concrete for industrial and commercial buildings, in particular the Larkin Co. Administration Building (1903) which was demolished in 1950. The building was designed to serve as the headquarters of a prosperous soap manufacturer, and to house its mail-order business. For the Larkin Company, Wright designed a facility for executives and departmental heads, as well as for the 1800 clerical staff.

The finished building, air-conditioned and light-filled, with dining facilities capable of serving 2000 people in shifts of up to 600 at lunch – Wright also designed eight-person dining tables with swivel tops that converted into benches for meetings – was ready for use in 1906.

RIGHT: Wright takes afternoon tea with members of the Taliesin Fellowship and their families.

BELOW: Wright at the drawing board, surrounded by students. His charismatic personality and personal brilliance attracted many aspiring architects to his several studios as apprentices. Both clients and colleagues often found him difficult and exacting, but most felt they had been enriched by the experience of working with him.

The overall design of the building and furnishings was based on utilitarian concerns: company head John D. Larkin had witnessed the great Chicago fire of 1871, and insisted that the building was fireproof. Wright therefore created a steel-framed building, clad in brick inside and out. Floors, desk tops, and cabinets were covered in magnesite, a chalky-gray substance which could be mixed, poured and troweled on the surfaces to enhance sound absorption.

Magnesite was also used for the sculptural decoration of the piers surrounding the central atrium, and was poured over a layer of felt flooring to give resistance, but under the weight of Wright's metal office furniture it soon chipped and cracked. All the office furniture for the main block was designed in metal for additional fireproofing, and included three different types of desks, four different types of chairs and a somewhat unstable three-legged chair that earned itself the nickname "the suicide chair" from Larkin employees. While Wright's metal furniture echoed the solid geometric exterior of the building, it also contrasted well with the light, airy and flexible open office space of the interior.

Earlier, in 1901, Wright had given a lecture at Chicago's Hull House entitled "The Art and Craft of the Machine," in which he had spoken of the important role

that new technology should play in American architecture. To add weight to his words, Wright unveiled his plans for the Prairie House, a design unlike any typical American house, which was regarded by Wright as one big box with little boxes inside. In the Prairie House design, Wright broke open the box, thus enabling physical and visual movement between the interior and exterior which was achieved by the use of light screens – long bands of continuous windows – and the removal of fixed interior-partition walls. These were replaced by head-height screens and built-in furniture that indicated, rather than compartmentalized, the possible uses for each space.

The years between 1905 and 1910 were the heyday of the Prairie House design, with some 40 being built. The adaptability of the design meant that Wright was able continually to revise possible approaches until 1936, when the Usonian House gradually emerged to provide inexpensive housing for average, middle-income families. Nevertheless, in the Usonian houses, Wright continued to give his clients individually designed houses and furniture, this time based on modular units. Hexagonal forms were used initially in the Paul R. and Jean S. Hanna House (1936), a design also known as the "Honeycomb House" because Wright believed that this shape was more economical than the more usual rectangle, and that it had a more natural, organic and therefore human quality.

The hexagonal form appears again in 1939 in the house and furniture designed for C. Leigh Stevens at

LEFT: An employee tests the circular elevator in the S. C. Johnson & Son Administration Building.

BELOW LEFT: Close-up detail of the glass tubes in the S. C. Johnson & Son Administration Building. The essence of this great industrial commission was light, enhanced by the use of these glass tubes, which were provided to Wright's specifications by the Corning Glass Works. Wright compared this 1936 building to his much earlier Larkin Building in Buffalo, New York.

RIGHT: Exterior view from the master-bedroom terrace at Fallingwater – the Edgar J. Kaufmann, Sr., House, which is generally considered Wright's masterwork. The terraces emphasize the horizontality of the structure, which is totally integral to its site.
.

Auldbrass Plantation, South Carolina. Later clients for Usonian houses again allowed Wright to demonstrate just how versatile the Usonian forms could be, and each house was indeed unique: it could be big or small; the grid could be hexagonal, rectangular, square, C-shaped or even L-planned, like the Sondern House (1940), for which Wright designed compact built-in furniture based on the same L-shaped modular unit used for the architecture.

Two of Wright's most renowned buildings from the 1930s, the Edgar J. Kaufmann, Sr. House, better known as Fallingwater, and the Administration Building for S. C. Johnson & Son, form the two extremes of Wright's efforts at establishing whole environments. Ever since his work on the Darwin D. Martin House and the Larkin Co. Administration Building of 1903, Wright had worked to link house-building with nature, and the creation of workplaces with the concept of religion. For Wright, the hearth was the moral and spiritual focus, while, in the workplace of the home, the use of tabular incriptions

LEFT: An overall view of Fallingwater on its wooded Pennsylvania site.

BELOW: Wright's drawing for the Solomon R. Guggenheim Museum, which was many years in the planning, due to the complexities of property acquisition and the New York City building code.

RIGHT: The architect pictured in contemplative mood. His own extensive writings on architecture and related subjects helped spread his design ideals to a wide public, in the United States and abroad.

(like the one in the Larkin Co. Administration Building entrance which read: "Honest labor needs no master, simple justice needs no slaves"), could bring the sacred into it. At the S. C. Johnson & Son Administration Building, Wright believed that the employees' attention should be concentrated entirely on their "sacred" work, and this led him to create a self-contained, hermetic environment that physically excluded the outside world. Employees were not to be distracted by views through windows; instead, light was filtered through a glass

THE MODERN GALLERY
MEMORIAL MUSEUM FOR THE SOLOMON R GUGGENHEIM FOUNDATION
FRANK LLOYD WRIGHT ARCHITECT

tubing supported by tall, slender, lily-pad-capped columns that tapered gently at their bases.

While this building represented Wright's interpretation of the sacramental place of work, Fallingwater represented his idea of a living place fused with nature. Straddling a small stream called Bear Run, Fallingwater is rooted to a ledge of rock and projects out as a free-floating platform over a small waterfall. Wright saw the cantilever construction of Fallingwater as echoing the way in which a tree supports its own network of branches. The concrete cantilevered planes of Fallingwater are held in place by walls of rough natural stone and inside, throughout the house, the table tops echo the cantilevered forms; three-legged chairs were used to provide extra stability on the irregular stone floors.

In the Solomon R. Guggenheim Museum in New York (1956), the building considered by many to be the climax of Wright's career (although it was not, in fact, the last project with which Wright was involved), all the structural and spatial principles and achievements that had concerned Wright throughout his 75 years as an architect, and that he had employed in Fallingwater, are combined here with the roof-lit containment of the S. C. Johnson & Son Administration Building. Once again, the organic nature of Wright's work is clear.

Frank Lloyd Wright Home, 1889 and Studio, 1895
Oak Park, Illinois

BELOW: The hearth in the drafting room
Its open plan allows for multiple use, and the fireplace mass
served the studio as a focal point around which activity flowed,
as in the house. Wright's own office opened to both the
reception hall and the drafting room.
Photograph by Jon Miller, © Hedrich-Blessing

LEFT: Built-in toy benches, geometric wall sconces and art
glass in the playroom, as well as a mural over the fireplace
designed by Wright and executed by Orlando Giannini
*Photograph by Ron Blunt, Courtesy of the Frank Lloyd Wright
Home and Studio Foundation, Oak Park, Illinois*

ABOVE: The dining room, making use of recessed lighting in the ceiling grille, patterned after oak leaves and branches
Photograph by Jon Miller, © Hedrich-Blessing

ABOVE RIGHT: Studio reception hall connecting the drafting room and library
Photograph by Jon Miller, © Hedrich-Blessing

RIGHT: Side chair, 1904, from the Frank Lloyd Wright Home and Studio, Oak Park, Illinois
Oak, leather upholstery, 40¼ H × 15 W × 18¾ D in.
Gift of the Sydney and Frances Lewis Foundation,
Virginia Museum of Fine Arts, Richmond, VA (85.74)

FAR RIGHT: Detail of the green-and-gold art-glass rectangles in the hall skylight
Photograph by Thomas A. Heinz

ABOVE: Barrel vault and ceiling grille in the playroom
Photograph by Jon Miller, © *Hedrich-Blessing*

LEFT: Entry foyer with plaster frieze and cornice
Photograph by Judith Bromley

William H. Winslow House, 1893
River Forest, Illinois

BELOW LEFT AND RIGHT: Both the frieze and the carved front door show patterns from nature rather than classical forms
Photographs by Thomas A. Heinz

BOTTOM RIGHT: Entry detail
Photograph by Thomas A. Heinz

BOTTOM LEFT: Drawing for the William H. Winslow House
© *The Frank Lloyd Wright Foundation*

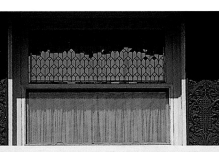

Nathan G. Moore House, 1895

Oak Park, Illinois

LEFT: The exterior shows Japanese-influenced design details, a feature that would recur in Wright's work throughout his 70-year career. The brickwork is in narrow Roman courses, like that of the William H. Winslow House on the preceding pages. The steeply pitched roofs would soon disappear from Wright's design repertoire in favor of the broad, low-lipped roofs of the later Prairie style. The Moore House was rebuilt above the first floor in 1923 after a fire.
Photograph by Balthazar Korab

BELOW: Detail from the ornamental front wall, which has weathered considerably since the house was built a century ago.
Photograph by Thomas A. Heinz

Ward W. Willits House, 1901

Highland Park, Illinois

BELOW LEFT: Spindle-backed chairs in the dining room create the feeling of "a room within a room"
Photograph by Balthazar Korab

RIGHT: Side chair, *c.* 1902
Oak with leather-covered slip-seat, 141½ × 43.3 × 45.8 cm
Victoria & Albert Museum, London, Purchased with the assistance of the National Art Collections Fund (W4-1992)

FAR RIGHT: The spindle-designed bannisters in the entry hall contributed to the sense of verticality, a function of the house's overall plan, which is cruciform with pyramidal massing. Characteristically, the compressive dimensions of the entry hall are succeeded by the spacious living area, with an end wall of floor-to-ceiling glass.
Photograph by Thomas A. Heinz

Arthur Heurtley House, 1902
Oak Park, Illinois

RIGHT: Arched entrance and horizontal brick courses on the exterior of this masterwork in the Prairie style give it an imposing presence, enhanced by the concrete stylobate that anchors the house to the site. The arched entrance is placed off-center to increase the sense of shelter, and expectation is heightened by the low walls flanking the entry, with their alternating courses of smooth and projecting bricks, varying from deep red to rose. Grace and contrast are provided by the expanses of glass on the second level, overhung by the gently sloping roof with its low chimney mass. Wright never repeated the dramatic treatment of the brickwork for this residence
Photograph by Balthazar Korab

BELOW: Arched fireplace in the living room of the Heurtley house echoes the entranceway and serves as the focal point for this spacious living area, with its pyramidal beamed ceiling
Photograph by Thomas A. Heinz

RIGHT: Living-room ceiling light executed to Wright's design by Chicago's Linden Glass Co. The pattern forms a silhouette of the house itself, viewed upside down
Photograph by Thomas A. Heinz

Susan Lawrence Dana House
(Dana-Thomas House), 1902
Springfield, Illinois

LEFT: Art glass and *The Moon Children*, a fountain by Richard Bock, adorn the reception area. The house was built for entertaining on a lavish scale and has the character of a public building in those areas not reserved for the immediate family. Its art glass is almost unparalleled for both extent and quality, with a color palette predominated by shades of yellow. All of its motifs were drawn from nature
Photograph by Doug Carr

BELOW: Exterior frieze displaying abstract patterns, which encircles the second floor
Photograph by Doug Carr

RIGHT: The arched ceiling panel and door surround, decorated in an abstracted butterfly theme – the only instance in which Wright employed a motif suggested by animal life rather than plant life
Photograph by Judith Bromley

BELOW: The gallery with print tables; behind, an art-glass "curtain" comprising nine free-hanging panels suspended on a wooden frame
Photograph by Judith Bromley

FACING PAGE, TOP: A sumac-inspired art-glass window, made by the Linden Glass Co., Chicago. A frequent collaborator with Wright, the glasshouse was so proud of its work for this residence that it figured in their advertising
Photograph by Doug Carr

FACING PAGE, BOTTOM: The sumac motif is repeated in the bedroom; it reappears throughout the house in ceiling fixtures, sconces, and table lamps
Photograph by Doug Carr

Larkin Co.
Administration Building, 1903

Buffalo, New York
(demolished 1950)

LEFT: Armchair, painted steel, 38 × 20¾ × 24¾ in.
Wright designed all the metal furniture and fittings for this
building, including the file cabinets built into the brick walls
below the high windows on the upper galleries
*Gift of Theodore R. Gamble, Jr., in honor of his mother, Mrs.
Theodore Robert Gamble, 1979,
The Metropolitan Museum of Art, New York, NY (1979.130)*

BELOW: Armchair, *c.* 1904-06
Painted steel, leather, 37½ H × 24¹¹⁄₁₆ W × 21⅛ D in.
The innovations devised for this first of Wright's commercial
commissions have affected office-building and -furniture
design to the present day
*Gift of The Sydney and Frances Lewis Foundation
Virginia Museum of Fine Arts, Richmond, VA (85.75)*

Darwin D. Martin House, 1904
Buffalo, New York

LEFT: Table, 1904, wood, 27 × 27 in.
Gift of Darwin R. Martin, 1968,
Albright-Knox Art Gallery, Buffalo, NY (68:9:1)

FACING PAGE: Stained-glass window pane, c. 1904,
41 × 25½ in.
Arlando Jiannini did the glass work for the house
Gift of Darwin R. Martin,
Albright-Knox Art Gallery, Buffalo, NY (68:9)

BELOW: Oversized urn in the grounds of the house, which were
elaborately landscaped, in keeping with the size and expense of
this ambitious project
Photograph by Balthazar Korab

Unity Temple, 1904

Oak Park, Illinois

BELOW LEFT: Sphere- and cube-shaped light fixtures overhang
the sanctuary, augmenting the natural light provided by
second-story windows and coffered skylights set with amber
glass
Photograph by Paul Rocheleau

BELOW RIGHT: Detail of the supporting columns formed, like
the walls, in concrete forms and subsequently washed to
expose the small-gravel aggregate. Massive piers at each corner
of the building echoed the monolithic effect of the columns
Photograph by Thomas A. Heinz

RIGHT: Poured-concrete exterior walls, columns and
architectural ornaments – a radical innovation that made
Unity Temple the first significant American architectural
statement in this medium
Photograph by Balthazar Korab

Frederick C. Robie House, 1906
Chicago, Illinois

FAR LEFT: French doors running the length of the living room bring the outdoors into this long, narrow living space on what was then a narrow suburban lot. The house unfolds along a single axis from the massive central core of the chimney
Photograph by Thomas A. Heinz

LEFT: Spindle-backed dining-room chairs contrast with the horizontal ceiling beams that bring the ceiling "down" to enhance the sense of shelter
Photograph by Paul Rocheleau

BELOW: George Mann Niedecken
Decorating scheme for living room, 1909-10
Pencil, watercolor on paper, 10¼ × 31¼ in.
Gift of Mr. and Mrs. Robert L. Jacobson,
Prairie Archives, Milwaukee Art Museum, WI (PA1977.1.1)

Avery Coonley House, 1907
Riverside, Illinois

BELOW LEFT: Desk for the Avery Coonley House, made by Niedecken and Walbridge, c. 1909
Oak, 45⅛ × 40¼ × 23⅞ in.
The Arts and Crafts influence is clear in the sensitive handling of a beautiful natural material, minimally adorned and wholly suited to its function
Gift of The Graham Foundation for Advanced Studies in the Fine Arts (1972.304)
Photograph © 1995, The Art Institute of Chicago, IL. All Rights Reserved

BELOW RIGHT: Avery Coonley Playhouse window featuring a stylized American flag and confetti. The exuberant use of art glass in the playhouse is one of its most attractive features
Seattle Art Museum, Seattle, WA (95.24)

TOP RIGHT: Rug detail showing the attention to design and color that made the Coonley house one of Wright's most fully coordinated and successful commissions. As he said of the project in his autobiography, "I put the best in me into the Coonley house"
Photograph by Thomas A. Heinz

FAR RIGHT: Wright's design for the first-floor hall rug, Avery Coonley House, 1908-11
Pencil, colored pencil on tracing paper, 8¾ × 9⅛ in.
Gift of Mr. and Mrs. Robert L. Jacobson,
Prairie Archives, Milwaukee Art Museum, WI (PA1977.2.29)
Copyright © 1995 The Frank Lloyd Wright Foundation

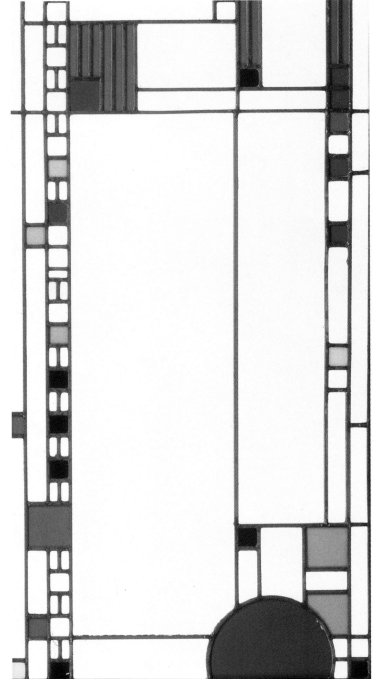

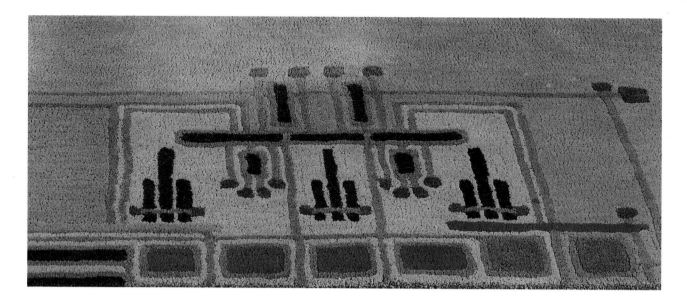

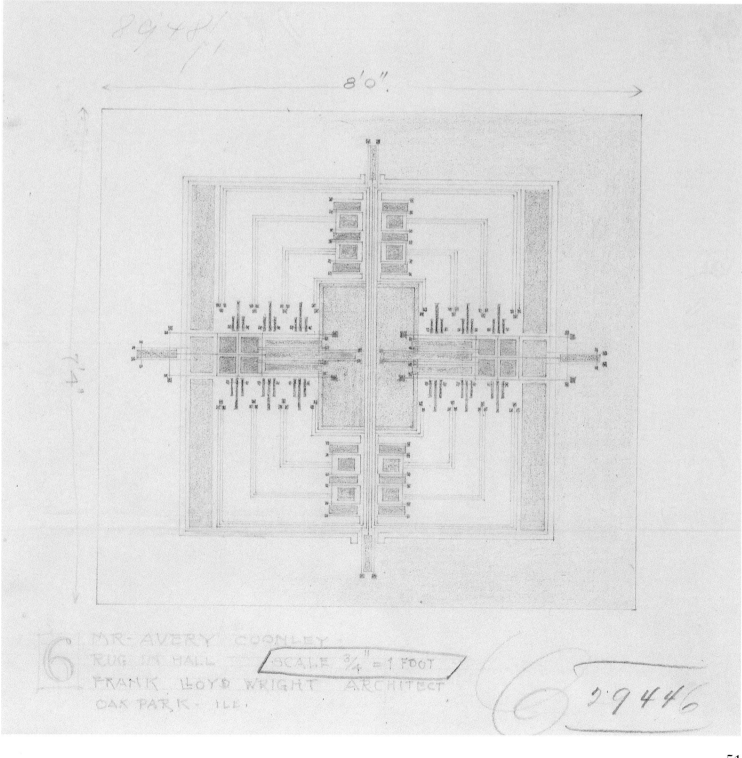

Meyer May House, 1908

Grand Rapids, Michigan

LEFT: Copper-framed art-glass windows and skylights surrounded by oak moldings create a serene and harmonious atmosphere in the living room, with its rich harvest colors
Photograph by Balthazar Korab

BELOW: Exterior ornamental copper façade contrasts with the massive brick and masonry tiers that seem to rise irresistably from the site
Photograph by Balthazar Korab

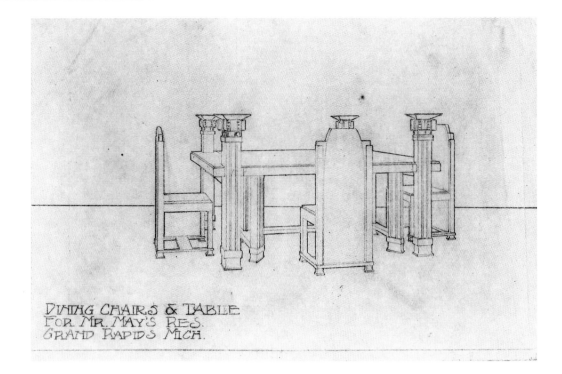

ABOVE: Frank Lloyd Wright and George Mann Niedecken
Design for dining table and chairs, *c.* 1910, Meyer May House,
Grand Rapids, Michigan
Pencil on tracing paper
Frank Lloyd Wright and Prairie School Collection,
Milwaukee Art Museum, WI

BELOW: The fireplace, with golden glass cemented into the
mortar joints
Photograph courtesy of Steelcase, Inc., Grand Rapids, MI

RIGHT: The four-posted dining-room table, and built-in planters
Photograph by Balthazar Korab

Francis W. Little House
(Northome), 1912

Wayzata, Minnesota
(demolished 1972)

LEFT: Installation of the living room of the Francis W. Little House in The American Wing, the Metropolitan Museum of Art, New York, NY

The 55-foot living room of this spacious Prairie-style house originally overlooked Minnesota's Lake Minnetonka and an inland view of the surrounding countryside. This was the second residence designed by Wright for Francis W. Little; the first was a brick home of T plan with a large stable in Peoria, Illinois (1902). Northome was Wright's first commission in Minnesota, and it is fortunate that this portion of an architectural landmark has been preserved from the demolition of 1972

Purchase, Bequest of Emily Crane Chadbourne, 1972 (1972.60.1), Installation through the generosity of Saul P. Steinberg and Reliance Group Holdings, Inc.

Midway Gardens, 1913

Chicago, Illinois
(demolished 1929)

RIGHT: Concrete "Sprite" sculpture, designed by Wright in collaboration with Alfonso Iannelli for the elaborate complex called Midway Gardens. It was a European-style beer garden intended to serve as a year-round cultural center just off Chicago's Midway. Its brick and patterned-concrete pavilions took shape amid considerable dissension among Wright and his creative collaborators on the project, and Midway Gardens operated at a loss from the outset. A Chicago brewer purchased it two years later, but Prohibition ended its use as a beer garden and the complex was razed.
Photograph by Thomas A. Heinz

Imperial Hotel, 1915-22

Tokyo, Japan
(demolished 1968)

BELOW: Mural over the hearth in the central foyer of the Imperial Hotel, one of the most ambitious projects of Wright's career. The richly ornamented building was constructed of native oya, a lava stone, and laid out on an axial plan, with guest rooms in the two wings and public rooms in the central area. The imposing multi-story lobby and every feature of the furnishings were designed by Wright, as well as the infrastructure that survived the great earthquake of 1923
Photograph by Ezra Stoller/ESTO Photographics

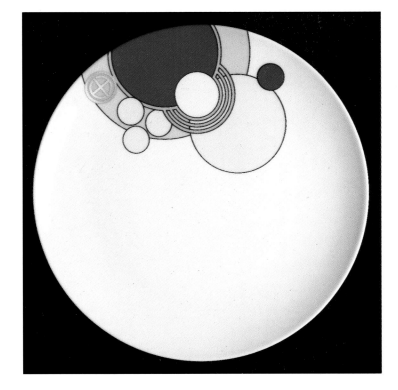

LEFT: Side chair, hexagonal back and seat covered in yellow oil cloth. More than 700 drawings were involved in the design for the Imperial Hotel and all its furnishings
Cooper-Hewitt Museum, New York, NY (1968-137-1)

RIGHT: Dinner plate from a service designed by Wright and manufactured by Noritake, Japan's pre-eminent porcelain manufacturer
Porcelain, diameter 10⅝ in.
Gift of Mr. and Mrs. Roger G. Kennedy, 1978,
The Metropolitan Museum of Art, New York, NY (1978.501.4)

BELOW: Porcelain place setting from the Cabaret Dinner Service created by Wright and used at the hotel's less formal dining room until 1933. (The service for the main dining room was of white porcelain with gold rims, handles, and design.)
Cooper-Hewitt Museum, New York, NY (1979-77-1 to 7)

Aline Barnsdall House
(Hollyhock House), 1917
Los Angeles, California

ABOVE: Poured-concrete sculptures and massive planters
command the view from the Olive Hill site
Photograph by Balthazar Korab

LEFT: The hearth and skylight in the living room: filtered light
from above is reflected in the pool that surrounds the fireplace
Photograph by Thomas A. Heinz

LEFT: Ornamental detail of the specially cast concrete piers. Originally, the entire structure was planned for reinforced poured concrete, but it was executed primarily in stucco on wood frame
Photograph by Balthazar Korab

BELOW: A gallery of hollyhock art glass carries out the dominant design theme in a composition of carefully controlled geometric forms
Photograph by Thomas A. Heinz

RIGHT: Dining-room chairs with hollyhock-motif backs complement the green-and-gold monochromatic color scheme of the principal living areas. The Japanese influence is apparent in this house, which was designed concurrently with the Imperial Hotel
Photograph by Balthazar Korab

Charles Ennis House, 1923
Los Angeles, California

LEFT: Exterior view of the house's textile-block construction, which gives it the monolithic presence of a pre-Columbian temple. To create the blocks, the concrete was precast into the hollow blocks on site, using local rock and sand. Steel rods were then interwoven in the hollow chambers of the blocks, which were set without mortar joints; instead, they were filled with grout or concrete for added strength. As they were not uniform, they proved difficult and expensive to lay up in walls, but the results were strikingly impressive
Photograph by Balthazar Korab

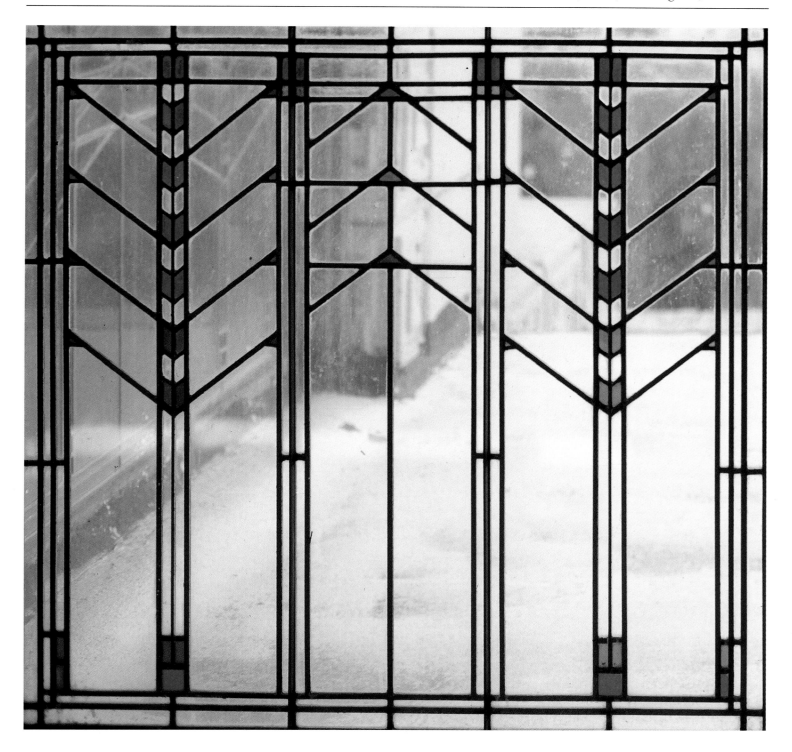

LEFT: Entry foyer, showing block piers and hearth surmounted
by a golden Tiffany mosaic of wisteria. Massive pottery and
bronze ceiling fixtures enhance the impressive colonnade
Photograph by Balthazar Korab

ABOVE: Art-glass windows framed by concrete blocks
lighten an interior that would be somber without the play of
color and light
Photograph by Thomas A. Heinz

John Storer House, 1923
Hollywood, California

ABOVE: The pool and terrace, overhung and surrounded by
tropical foliage
Photograph by Balthazar Korab

LEFT: Living room, with plain, patterned, and pierced concrete
blocks that show both Mayan and Japanese influence and
Wright's favorite classical sculpture, *Winged Victory*
Photograph by Balthazar Korab

Taliesin, 1925-59

Spring Green, Wisconsin

TOP LEFT: The "bird walk" that extends from the living room to provide the feeling of a tree house over the ambient countryside
Photograph by Thomas A. Heinz

BELOW LEFT: The living room, with its colorful carpet, is a memorable, multilevel space with contrasting surfaces of native limestone, burnished wood, and textured plaster. Indirect and clerestory-window lighting enhance the serene feeling. The barrel chairs reflect the circles in the carpet and on the upper wall
Photograph by Thomas A. Heinz

BELOW: The curtain in Taliesin's Hillside Theater, designed by Wright and executed by his apprentices
Photograph by Balthazar Korab

Arizona Biltmore Hotel, 1927

Phoenix, Arizona

LEFT: Exterior view showing block detail and sconce
Photograph by Balthazar Korab

BELOW: Integral block sculpture, decorative planter, and light
fixture on the elegantly landscaped grounds of the historic
luxury hotel
Photograph by Thomas A. Heinz

LEFT: Block ornament and light fixtures in the dining room set off the floor-to-ceiling windows and the gold-leaf ceiling with its triangular insets. The hotel has been referred to since its construction as "the Jewel of the Desert"
Photograph by Balthazar Korab

ABOVE: Lighted blocks set in decorative piers in the foyer, and a geometrical art-glass mural designed by Frank Lloyd Wright, entitled *Saguaro Forms and Cactus Flowers*
Photograph by Balthazar Korab

Edgar J. Kaufmann, Sr. House
(Fallingwater), 1935
Mill Run, Pennsylvania

LEFT: Windows along the north elevation with the mitered
corners pioneered by Wright to fulfill his intention of turning
exterior walls into "screens" between inner and outer spaces.
Regarded as his masterwork, Fallingwater is perhaps the most
widely admired structure of modern times
Photograph by Paul Rocheleau

ABOVE: Exterior stair detail
Photograph by Paul Rocheleau

LEFT: Portable seating, a large ceiling grille, and a massive hearth. Bright notes of color like the Cherokee red window outlines and fireplace accessories contrast with the prevailing colors of sandstone and concrete in a harmonious shade of chamois in the stone-flagged living room
Photograph by Thomas A. Heinz

BELOW: The living-room hearth, formed by a boulder on the site, serves as a focal point for the 1800-square-foot space
Photograph by Thomas A. Heinz

Paul R. and Jean S. Hanna House
(Honeycomb House), 1936
Stanford, California

LEFT: Exterior view of the Usonian Honeycomb House, built to the slope of the hill. Japanese in feeling, the house has many window walls that swing open to the concrete terraces and gardens. The hexagonal design unit allowed for a free flow of space that could be freely adapted to the needs of a growing family. Note the perforated overhang above the entrance, echoed by the open grillework below it
Photograph by Balthazar Korab

BELOW: The furniture in the living room, emphasizing the hexagonal "honeycomb" building units with which the house was designed
Photograph by Ezra Stoller/ESTO Photographics

Herbert Jacobs House I, 1936
Madison, Wisconsin

ABOVE: Simple clerestory panels, brickwork, clear glass, and natural wood were featured throughout this first of Wright's Usonian houses, designed to be affordable and efficient for contemporary families without compromising beauty. The Jacobs helped to construct the house, which was built on a concrete slab and heated by pipes buried in the floor.
Photograph by Paul Rocheleau

RIGHT: "Living kitchen" area and brick hearth – a concept central to Usonian designs, which eliminated the formal dining room and placed the kitchen at the core of the house
Photograph by Paul Rocheleau

S. C. Johnson & Son
Administration Building, 1936
and Research Tower, 1944
Racine, Wisconsin

LEFT: Reception area with circular, glass-tube ceiling. Wright struck a new note in commercial architecture in this landmark complex designed to provide a spacious, light-filled, and congenial working environment
Photograph by Ezra Stoller/ESTO Photographics

BELOW: Building exterior showing glass-tube design produced to Wright's specifications by New York's Corning Glass Works
Photograph by Thomas A. Heinz

LEFT: Reception area, featuring curved walls and glass-encased lighting. The innovative construction techniques employed here created unexpected delays and cost overruns, but Herbert F. Johnson and his employees were more than happy with the results
Photograph by Balthazar Korab

ABOVE: Lab area, with its curved elevator and tube-encircled workspace
Photograph by Ezra Stoller/ESTO Photographics

RIGHT: The "great workroom," showing the mushroom-shaped, dendriform columns that support the roof and allow the exterior walls to function primarily as a light-screen
Photograph by Balthazar Korab

ABOVE: The office furniture was designed by Wright and was executed by Racine's Metal Office Furniture Company, the forerunner of Steelcase Inc. Wright's mandate to create a total work environment resulted in a new kind of office furniture that echoed the lines of the building, complemented and brightened the interior, and helped employees carry out their tasks efficiently
Photograph courtesy of Steelcase, Inc., Grand Rapids, MI

Herbert F. Johnson House
(Wingspread), 1937
Wind Point, Wisconsin

ABOVE: Exterior view showing the observation deck and
clerestory windows
Photograph by Thomas A. Heinz

LEFT: The library area features Wright's built-in sofa, coffee
tables, and octagonal ottomans. The great curved chimney is
the focal point of the living space, with its warm brick and oak
tones enriched by natural light from above. At right is part of
the curved staircase that leads up to the observation point
requested by client Herbert F. Johnson
Photograph by Balthazar Korab

ABOVE: Large flower urn
Photograph by Thomas A. Heinz

BELOW: Aerial view of Wingspread, showing the "wings"
leading off the central core to create a pinwheel effect
Photograph by Thomas A. Heinz

ABOVE: Front and back view of the Wright-designed chairs
Collection of Richard Rasnick

BELOW: Spiral steps leading from the mezzanine to the
observation deck
Photograph by Thomas A. Heinz

Taliesin West, 1937-59

Scottsdale, Arizona

RIGHT: The windows and hearth follow the triangular motif drawn from the surrounding mountains. Wright's western retreat evolved into a complex of buildings linked by covered walkways, terraces, and courtyards that drew their inspiration from the awe-inspiring desert mesa site. Originally roofed with canvas, the complex was later roofed with permanent materials.
Photograph by Ezra Stoller/ESTO Photographics

BELOW: Massive masonry with rubble stone from the desert floor looms over the geometric form at the entrance
Photograph by Balthazar Korab

ABOVE: The ceiling gives the theater a tent-like atmosphere. Concerts were often given at the home/studio, as they were in Wright's Wisconsin retreat. His passion for music was lifelong
Photograph by Thomas A. Heinz

LEFT: The living room is dominated by the rugged masonry hearth and framed by the redwood forms that uphold the ceiling panels. Native American designs and natural materials had a place of honor at Taliesin West, which seems at once primitive, like the original Ocotillo camps, and highly refined
Photograph by Balthazar Korab

Annie Pfeiffer Chapel,
Florida Southern College, 1938
Lakeland, Florida

LEFT: The chapel's vertical thrust makes it highly visible on the low-scale. Its spare and spacious interior recalls that of Unity Temple and fosters a close connection between speaker and congregation
Photograph by Balthazar Korab

BELOW LEFT: Stairwell and wall studded with colored glass to refract the tropical sunlight and contrast with the primary construction material of reinforced concrete blocks
Photograph by Balthazar Korab

BELOW RIGHT: The double-triangle skylight, set above intricate geometric blocks, is the chapel's primary light source. Originally, Wright intended to filter the overhead light through hanging plants in concrete planters, but the plan proved unworkable
Photograph by Balthazar Korab

C. Leigh Stevens House
(Auldbrass Plantation), 1939
Yemassee, South Carolina

LEFT: Side chair and triangular end tables
Plycore with cyprus veneer; chestnut naugahyde upholstery
Chair: 28 × 21 × 28 in.; End tables: 17⅝ × 30 × 30 in.,
22⅜ × 26⅛ × 18¼ in.
Gift of Jessica Stevens Loring, 1981 (1981.438.2-.4)
The Metropolitan Museum of Art, New York, NY

BOTTOM LEFT: The library, with its angular furniture and
pitched ceiling of tidewater cypress planks
Photograph by Paul Rocheleau

BELOW: The living room, which features strong geometric
shapes and clerestories. This Usonian house was built on a
hexagonal module
Photograph by Paul Rocheleau

Unitarian Church, 1947

Shorewood Hills, Wisconsin

LEFT: The congregation of this Unitarian church 36 miles from Taliesin was eager to have Wright design its church, and he spent much time on the project. The structure consists of a larger and smaller triangle adjoined. The sanctuary is situated at the apex of the larger triangle, which opens to the smaller for social gatherings
Photograph by Balthazar Korab

BELOW: The steeply pitched copper roof rises like a prow over the windowed sanctuary
Photograph by Balthazar Korab

William Palmer House, 1950

Ann Arbor, Michigan

BELOW: Triangular forms in the living room merge house and furniture under the richly toned cypress ceiling. The living area projects dramatically into the landscaped garden. Muted gold, green, and amber upholstery tones are counterpointed in the Japanese textiles on the dining chairs
Photograph by Balthazar Korab

RIGHT: Pierced-brick blocks allow additional light to filter in, reflected in the waxed red floor tiles. Simple pottery and metalware accessories are in harmony with their setting
Photograph by Balthazar Korab

Isadore J. Zimmerman House, 1950
Manchester, New Hampshire

FACING PAGE: The living room, showing the quartet music stand, based on one used at Taliesin, with colored-glass detail in the foreground
Photograph by Paul Rocheleau

LEFT: Quartet music stand and stools, 1950. The Zimmermans were accomplished musicians who played the violin, cello, and piano. Their friends often gathered at their home to share their love of music
Bequest of Isadore J. and Lucille Zimmerman,
The Currier Gallery of Art, Manchester, NH
Photograph by Bill Finney

BELOW: Dining-room table with chairs, 1950
All the furniture is economical and flexible without compromising quality
Bequest of Isadore J. and Lucille Zimmerman,
The Currier Gallery of Art, Manchester, NH
Photograph by Bill Finney

Harold C. Price Co. Tower, 1952
Bartlesville, Oklahoma

ABOVE: A signed tile, situated near the entrance of the tower
Courtesy, the Phillips Petroleum Company

LEFT: Mural on the nineteenth floor, designed by Wright
Courtesy, the Phillips Petroleum Company

BELOW LEFT: Detail showing copper stamping
Courtesy, the Phillips Petroleum Company

BELOW RIGHT: Exterior view, featuring the copper-faced
parapets, louvers, and gold-tinted glass
Courtesy, the Phillips Petroleum Company

Beth Sholom Synagogue, 1954
Elkins Park, Pennsylvania

LEFT: The synagogue's pyramidal design is suspended from a concrete-and-steel tripod, eliminating the need for internal support. The tripod rises from three main concrete masses at ground level and supports sloped glass screens that comprise the greater part of the structure
Photograph by Balthazar Korab

BELOW: Exterior detail, repeating the triangular motif in the incised oiled walnut trim inset with Hebrew inscriptions
Photograph by Paul Rocheleau

ABOVE: Exterior detail featuring designs of the menorah
stamped in aluminum, steel and glass. A cantilevered canopy
overhangs the main entrance
Photograph by Balthazar Korab

LEFT: The light coming in from the translucent pyramid
changes from silver to gold during the course of the day. At
night the synagogue radiates light. It has been designated by
the American Institute of Architects as one of 17 Wright
buildings to be retained as an example of his contribution to
American culture
Photograph by Paul Rocheleau

Gerald B. Tonkens House, 1954
Amberly Village, Ohio

RIGHT: The ceiling and hearth surround illustrate Wright's use of the "Usonian Automatic" building system, here using a two-foot-square module with the standard wall-block surface two feet by one foot. One wall of the core, which contains heating and cooling elements, is the living room fireplace. Pierced blocks admit light to the workspace core as a clerestory. All the woodwork and furniture is of Philippine mahogany. The house crowns a knoll on its wooded six-acre property and is considered a major exponent of Wright's Usonian style
Photograph by Paul Rocheleau

ABOVE: View from the terrace showing exterior block-and-glass construction. The house is of L-plan design, with the living room, extended by a lanai, in the shorter leg and sleeping quarters and study in the larger. The 90-degree turn occurs around the work space
Photograph by Paul Rocheleau

LEFT: Built-in sideboards and cupboard in the dining room, where the wall and ceiling block pattern contrasts with the delicate Japanese prints
Photograph by Paul Rocheleau

Annunciation
Greek Orthodox Church, 1956
Wauwatosa, Wisconsin

RIGHT: The Byzantine-inspired circular forms and arches of this house of worship are based on a ground plan in the form of a Greek cross. The second level comprises a bowl-shaped balcony that is covered by the dome of the roof, the whole supported on ambient arches. Broad, shallow steps fan out before the main entrance under its projecting archway. The massive urn-crowned pedestals left and right of the stairway help to anchor the structure to the site
Photograph by Balthazar Korab

Solomon R. Guggenheim
Museum, 1956

New York, New York

BELOW LEFT: The continuously spiraling ramp around the main gallery was designed to lead the visitor from the upper level, reached by elevator, down to the ground-floor atrium. A continuous band of skylights, supplemented by incandescent light sources, follows the curve of the wall to illuminate the paintings
Photograph by Alan Detrick/New England Stock

BELOW AND BOTTOM: Interior views of the museum's original galleries
Photographs by Paul Warchol

Marin County Civic Center, 1957
San Raphael, California

BELOW: Roof detail, with spherical ornamentation recurring above and below. The complex includes an Administration Building and Hall of Justice of similar concrete form with metal roofs. Each long arched wing moves out toward a distant hill. These were the only government buildings executed by Wright, although others reached the design stage
Photograph by Balthazar Korab

RIGHT: Radio tower pylon and exterior view
Photograph by Balthazar Korab

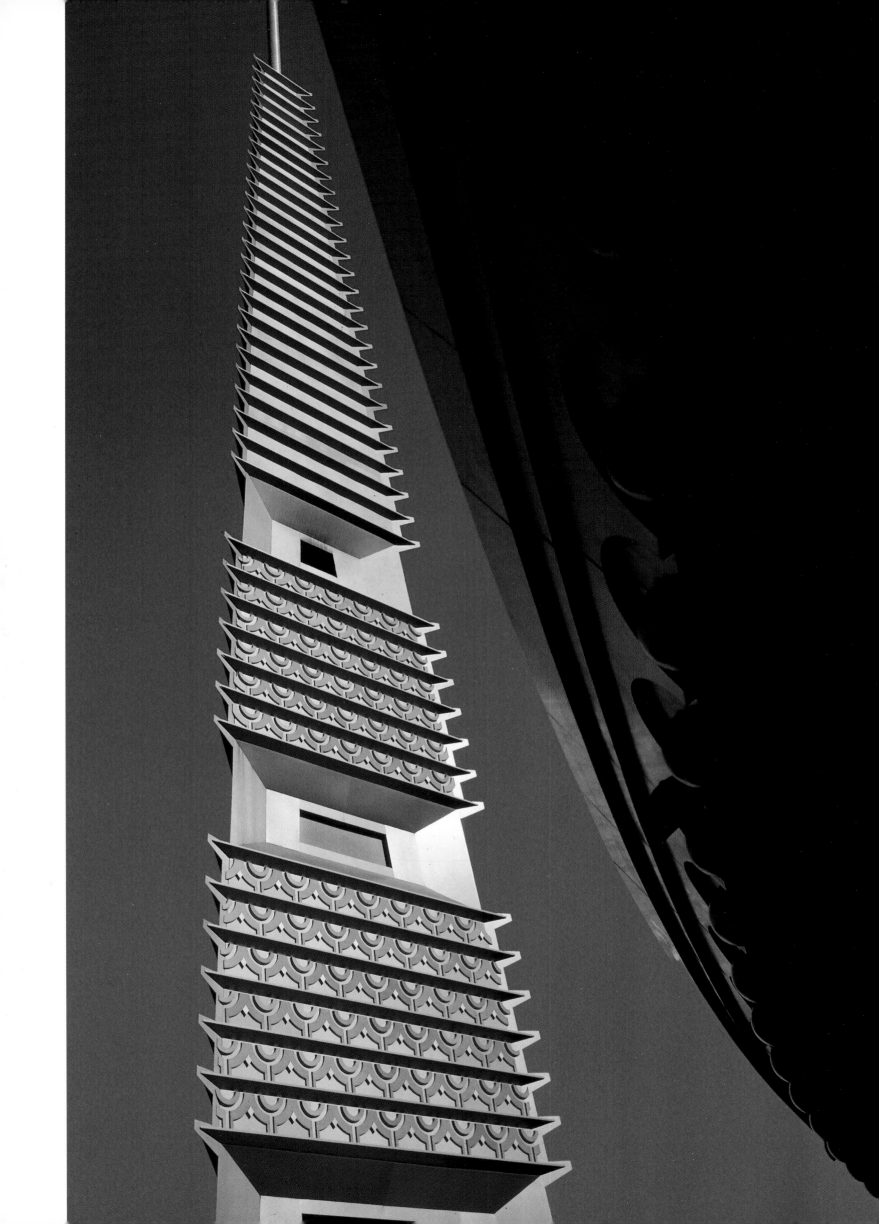

Grady Gammage Memorial Auditorium, 1959
Arizona State University

Tempe, Arizona

LEFT: Pedestrian bridge, with its repetitive circular motif
Photograph by Balthazar Korab

BELOW: Detail of the exterior, with slender columns topped by spheres
Photograph by Balthazar Korab

Acknowledgments

The publisher wishes to thank Martin Bristow, the designer; Sara Dunphy, the picture researcher; Clare Haworth-Maden, the editor; Simon Shelmerdine for production; and the museums and individuals listed below for supplying the illustrations:

Albright-Knox Art Gallery, Buffalo, NY/Gift of Mr. Darwin R. Martin (69:9:1), (68:9): pages 44, 45 (top)

The Bettmann Archive: pages 10 (top), 21

Ron Blunt/Courtesy the Frank Lloyd Wright Home and Studio Foundation: pages 22-23

Judith Bromley: pages 8 (right), 11 (bottom), 26, 40 (both)

Buffalo and Erie County Historical Society, Buffalo, NY: page 16

Doug Carr: pages 4, 38-39, 39, 41 (both)

© **1995 The Art Institute of Chicago, Chicago, IL. All Rights Reserved/Gift of Mr. and Mrs. F. M. Fahrenwald (1971.749), Photograph by Jon Gronkowski Photography:** page 7 (top left)/© **1993, Gift of the Graham Foundation for Advanced Studies in the Fine Arts (1972.304):** page 50 (left)

Cooper-Hewitt Museum, New York, NY: pages 13, 60, 61 (bottom)

The Currier Gallery of Art, Manchester, NH/Bequest of Isadore J. and Lucille Zimmerman/Photographs by Bill Finney: page 109 (both)

© **Hedrich Blessing/Photographs by Jon Miller:** pages 7 (top right), 9 (top left), 23, 24, 25 (top), 27

Thomas A. Heinz: pages 1, 14 (bottom), 15 (top and bottom right), 18 (bottom), 25 (bottom right), 28 (top), 29 (both), 31, 33, 36-37, 37, 46 (right), 48 (top), 51 (top), 58, 62, 64 (bottom), 69, 72 (both), 75, 80-81, 81, 87, 93, 94 (both), 95 (bottom), 99

Balthazar Korab: pages 2, 30, 32 (left), 34-35, 45 (bottom), 47, 52, 53, 55, 63, 64 (top), 65, 66-67, 68, 70, 71, 73, 74, 76, 77, 82-83, 88, 91, 92, 96, 98-99, 100, 101 (both), 104, 105, 106, 107, 112-113, 115, 120-21, 124, 125, 126, 127

The Metropolitan Museum of Art, New York, NY/Gift of Mr. and Mrs. Roger G. Kennedy, 1978 (1978.501.6) (1978.501.4): pages 14 (top), 61 (top)/**Gift of Theodore R. Gamble, Jr., in honor of his mother, Mrs. Theordore Robert Gamble, 1979 (1979.130):** pages 42/**Purchase, Bequest of Emily Crane Chadbourne, 1972 (1972.60.1), Installation through the generosity of Saul P. Steinberg and Reliance Group Holdings, Inc.:** pages 56-57/**Gift of Jessica Stevens Loring, 1981 (1981.438.2-.4]:** page 102 (top)

New England Stock/Photograph by Alan Detrick: pages 122-123

Courtesy the Phillips Petroleum Company: pages 110, 111 (all three)

Prairie Archives, Milwaukee Art Museum, Milwaukee, WI: page 54 (top)/**Gift of Mr. and Mrs. Robert L. Jackson (PA1977.1.1.):** pages 48-49/**Gift of Mr. and Mrs. Robert L. Jackson (PA1977.2.29),** © **The Frank Lloyd Wright Foundation:** pages 51 (bottom)

Richard Rasnick: page 95 (top)

Paul Rocheleau: pages 8 (left), 9 (top right and bottom), 11 (top), 46 (left), 49, 78, 79, 84, 84-85, 102 (bottom), 103, 108, 113, 114, 116-117, 118, 119

Seattle Art Museum, Seattle, WA: page 50 (right)

Steelcase Inc., Grand Rapids, MI: pages 54 (bottom), 90

© **Ezra Stoller/ESTO Photographics:** pages 15 (bottom left), 17 (bottom), 59, 83, 86-87, 89, 96-97

UPI/Bettmann Newsphotos: pages 6, 7 (bottom), 10 (bottom), 12 (both), 17 (top), 18 (top), 20 (bottom)

Courtesy of the Trustees of the Victoria & Albert Museum, London: page 32 (right)

Virginia Museum of Fine Arts, Richmond, Va: page 43/**Gift of the Sydney and Frances Lewis Foundation (85.74):** page 25 (bottom right)

Paul Warchol: page 123 (both)

© **Western Pennsylvania Conservancy:** pages 19, 20 (top)

© **The Frank Lloyd Wright Foundation:** page 28 (bottom)